Helping Children See Jesus

ISBN: 978-1-933206-65-3

No Tree For Christmas
and
Peggy's Christmas Stocking

Author: Rose-Mae Carvin
Illustrator: Frances Hertzler
Computer Graphic Artist: Jonathan Ober
Typesetting and Layout: Morgan Melton, Patricia Pope

© 2017 Bible Visuals International
PO Box 153, Akron, PA 17501-0153
Phone: (717) 859-1131
www.biblevisuals.org

All rights reserved. No part of this publication may be reproduced, stored in a retrieval system or transmitted in any form by any means, electronic, mechanical, photocopy, recording or otherwise, without the prior permission of the publisher, except as provided by USA copyright law.

For a group-setting format of this story and other related items, please visit our web store at shop.biblevisuals.org and search using "5365".

Who His own self bare our sins in His own body on the tree, that we, being dead to sins, should live unto righteousness: by Whose stripes ye are healed.
1 Peter 2:24

It is more blessed to give than to receive. Acts 20:35b

NO TREE FOR CHRISTMAS

An 'it-really-truly-happened' story

Show Illustration #1

It was Christmas Eve and the little house on the city street was filled with delicious smells. A big cake stood on the kitchen table where five busy children could pause from time to time and admire it. The frosting swirled higher and higher like gobs of whipped cream. Tiny colored candies set it all a-glitter. Warm mince pies were cooling on top of the oven and cookies were crowding each other for room in the cookie jar.

Show Illustration #2

Bill stood with his hand on the door knob sniffing the wonderful smells. Then, impatiently, he said, "Mother, come on. Please! Don't you think you've waited long enough to get a tree? Prob'ly won't get a thing now, waiting so long just because they'd be cheaper."

Mother motioned in his direction and went on giving orders to the four little girls. "Remember, " she said, "Beth is the oldest. You all do as she says. And, Rose Mae, be sure to let Mary help you set the table. She is six now and big enough to help. And, please, all of you, don't let Ruthie get into trouble." Winding a long curl around her finger, Mother gave five-year-old Ruthie a hug. "We'll be back in plenty of time for supper," she said.

As Bill stood watching, he was thinking that if Father were living there would have been a tree out in the garage right now, waiting to be trimmed. Perhaps he should have insisted Mother buy one sooner, since he was the only one in the family to take Father's place. He *had* tried, but Mother would not listen.

Of course, Mother had to be careful how she spent money. Yet she did always manage to get the things they needed. She really was a wonderful mother. But this time she had gone too far. Those girls would be terribly disappointed if they did not have a tree.

Show Illustration #3

Only last night Rose Mae had prayed for one. How would they explain to a seven-year-old about prayer, if they could not get a tree? Beth was only nine, but she was sensible. She would understand.

Bill was thinking of these things, his hand still on the door knob when he felt a hand on his. "Well come on, Son," Mother was saying, "I am ready now." And Bill's mother turned his hand so that the door opened as she smiled up at him. "How did you ever get to be so tall?" she asked.

Bill noticed how much larger his hand was than his mother's. He pushed his straight hair up under his woolen cap and took his mother's arm. *How tiny she is*, he thought.

Show Illustration #4

Down the long city street, Bill and his mother walked. At each place where Christmas trees had been for sale, they stopped. Yet they could see before they got there that there were no trees for sale now. On and on they went. It was always the same. All the trees had been sold. Only broken branches lay on the ground.

"Let's pick these up, Bill," Mother said. "They will make nice decorations."

"Guess we might as well," Bill said in a tired voice. "They are all the Christmas tree we'll have this year. Let's go back home and tell the girls."

"Not yet, son, not yet. Just a little farther. We may find one yet." Mother was remembering Rose Mae's prayer. They walked more slowly now.

Show Illustration #5

Suddenly Bill heard his mother say, "Look, Bill! Look over there! That man has *one* tree left. Let's hurry over. He is getting ready to leave. It's not a very pretty tree. I guess that's why he could not sell it. But we can fix it up. Hurry!"

Mother was out of breath from running and talking at the same time. But she had a big smile and her eyes were shining as she said, "Merry Christmas, Sir! I suppose you would be willing to sell this tree cheap since it is the last one you have, and not very nice?"

"No Ma'am!" the man answered.

"Did you say, 'No Ma'am'?" Mother's voice shook.

"Yes'm, I said, 'No Ma'am.' That's what I said."

"But why? Why is it not for sale?"

"Because it's for my own children. That's why. I had to save *one*. Sold the best ones. Trees were scarce this year. We'll have to be satisfied with this one."

"And you won't sell it for any price?"

"No Ma'am. Can't disappoint my children. They expect me to bring a tree home. They're waiting for me now. Good-bye. Hope you find a tree, Ma'am." The man picked up the scrawny little tree and walked away.

Tears were in Mother's eyes as she said, "You were right, Bill. I waited too long. We shall have no tree. Next time I'll listen to you, Son."

Bill put his arm around his mother's shoulders. "Never mind, Mom. You did what you thought was best. Come on. Let's go home. I'll try to make the girls understand."

Show Illustration #6

Four heads were at the window when Bill and his mother got home. They looked like steps, Bill decided.

Low in the left hand corner of the window they could see little Ruthie's curly head. She was the first step. She was smiling and Bill could see her big dimples through the window.

The second step was made by Mary's head. Her lovely dark hair and eyes shone clearly, as she waited patiently.

Rose Mae's head made the third step. Bill saw that she was not looking at him, nor at their mother. Her eyes were fastened on the empty space behind him, where a tree should have been as he dragged it along–the tree for which she had prayed.

The highest step belonged to Beth. *She's kinda bossy sometimes*, Bill thought, *but she sure is a help to Mother. She'll be more disappointed for the others than for herself.*

Bill heard Rose Mae cry, "They don't have a tree! We aren't going to have a Christmas tree!"

The four steps disappeared quickly. The door was thrown open wide. "Where's the tree? Where's the tree?" four young voices rang out in disappointment. And four pairs of brown eyes looked accusingly at their mother.

Bill made a motion with his hand and they stepped aside to let their mother and him through the door. "Couldn't you get a tree, Mother?" Beth asked gently.

Mother just shook her head, "No." The children saw that she was crying and stood silently by, a disappointed, unhappy little family.

Bill made the girls sit down as he explained what had happened. "So we have no tree, " he ended. "But look at everything else we have. For one thing, look at how healthy we all are. And I'm hungry. Supper ready, Beth?"

Show Illustration #7

They *were* a healthy family, as Bill had said. It was Rose Mae's turn to say grace. When she had finished the usual "thank You" to God for food, she added, "I asked Thee for a tree, dear God. Didn't You hear me? Never mind about it now, 'cause it's too late. But I was sure You'd help Mommy find a tree. Amen."

"*It isn't too late*," Mother said when Rose Mae had finished praying. "It isn't too late at all. God can still send us a tree, and somehow I think He is going to."

"Ah, please Mom, don't start that again," Bill said. "Don't get their hopes up *again*."

"Well, I'm not saying that God *will*, exactly. I am only saying God could–and He might," Mother explained.

Bill just shook his head.

After the children had prepared for bed, they gathered around their mother as she read the Christmas story. Bill noticed that Mother did not stop at the birth of Jesus. She turned pages in her Bible and read about His death and resurrection, without pausing. When she had finished reading, he understood why.

"The Christmas story is not complete without the story of WHY Christ Jesus was born," Mother said in a quiet voice. "And please remember, each of you, that the cross of the Lord Jesus was really a tree–a much more important tree than any we could have had for Christmas. Without it, Christmas would have been in vain." Bill saw tears in Rose Mae's eyes as she gave their mother a little hug.

"Now off to bed with you, every one," Mother said after they had all prayed. "I'll be up soon. I'll just trim the room with these branches Bill and I picked up."

Branches...Branches! Bill thought. That was it! The branches! He could make a tree from those branches. He was sure he could.

Bill was so excited he could scarcely wait for the others to go upstairs. "I'll stay up a while and help you, Mother."

"All right, Son," Mother said. "Beth, please tuck these sleepy-heads in for me tonight. Bill will help me here and then we shall come to bed. Everyone will be up early tomorrow."

Mother waited only until the last little head had disappeared from the room before she spoke: "What is it, Son? Why are you so excited?"

"Just you wait and see, Madam!" Bill's eyes shone. "If you will let me do as I want to do, I think we'll have a tree yet."

Show Illustration #8

Bill's mother watched as he raced to the porch. When he returned he had her old broom. "Hold this, Mother, will you please?" Bill's excitement was contagious. He whisked out his pen knife and without even asking permission, started cutting notches in the handle. He took thin wire and wired the branches of evergreen into the notches. Together they wound brown crepe paper to cover the handle. Then Bill ran down the steps to the basement, bringing a bucket of coal back with him. Mother watched in surprise, as Bill put the sweeping end of the broom deep inside the bucket of coal and covered the bucket with brown paper. He stood the bucket with its home-made brown tree in a corner of the room. Then they both sat down and laughed and cried together.

"Who ever heard of a broom tree before? " Bill asked.

"Yes, who ever did?" Mother laughed.

"Well we've heard of it now," Bill said. "It sure looks kinda straggly. But I'll bet those girls will think it's about the most beautiful tree they ever saw."

And they did!

Show Illustration #9

What fun the girls had the next morning trimming the broom tree. Bill hung their favorite angel on top. "I can see it better when it isn't up high like it usually is," Mary said.

Ruthie stood and made faces at herself in the shiny balls hanging on the lowest branches.

As the early morning sun shone in through the window, it seemed to light up the simple little home-made tree, mixing the colors of the bright ornaments all together. "It is! It is! It really is the loveliest tree we have ever had," Rose Mae declared. "God did answer my prayer, Mommy. He did!"

"Yes, dear," Mother said, holding her small daughter close. "God put the idea for the broom tree in your brother's mind. Sometimes He answers our prayers by showing us what we can do for ourselves."

Show Illustration #10

Bill stood silently watching his mother and sisters. Slowly, hesitating between each word, he said, "Well, if you think that idea was pretty good, I wonder if you'd like to hear another idea I have."

"Of course, we'd like to hear it, Son, " Mother said. "What is this other idea?"

"Well," Bill said, "I've been thinking how, before Jesus went back to Heaven, He told His disciples to go into all the world and preach the Gospel. And I've been thinking we ought to do something special to show our appreciation for all that we have." All the family sat quietly listening. This was quite a speech for their usually silent Bill to be making.

Bill continued, "And I've been thinking about something else. The best way we can help to do as Jesus said–preach the Gospel all over the world– is by praying and giving money. How would it be if we made some paper trees to look like my beautiful broom tree?" Bill smiled as he waved his hand toward the home-made tree.

Beth was watching Bill, her big brown eyes wide with questions. But she said nothing. But this wasn't so for Rose Mae. She could wait silently no longer. "Whatever for, Bill?" she questioned. "What would we do with paper trees?"

Mother motioned for Rose Mae to be quiet as Bill continued. "I thought we might begin doing without things we really don't need, like ice cream cones and candy suckers 'n things, and paste the money to the paper trees. That way we could have fun trimming our little trees and we could save money to help the missionaries preach the Gospel."

Bill sat down quickly. He was afraid his sisters might not like the idea. He was surprised when Rose Mae said, "That's a good idea, Bill. Let's do it!"

Show Illustration #11

Mary hurried off to her room and came back with green paper and scissors. Mother helped them all cut out paper trees. Then each one seemed to remember a penny, or a nickel, or dime which they had been saving for something special. Soon each paper tree had at least one ornament on it.

And guess what! Before long other boys and girls who heard the story of the broom tree were using paper trees and scotch-taping money to them to be used for missionaries in many places of the world. And countless boys and girls in other lands were hearing the story of the Lord Jesus Who died for them, because of the money those boys and girls gave–because of the things they did without, so that they could give.

Bill is a big man now. He will be very happy when he reads this story and knows what boys and girls are doing because God gave him the idea for a broom tree.

PEGGY'S CHRISTMAS STOCKING

Show Illustration #1

Peggy was only three years old. So she could not *remember* much about other Christmas days when she was tiny. But Peggy was sure that she knew all about Christmas just the same.

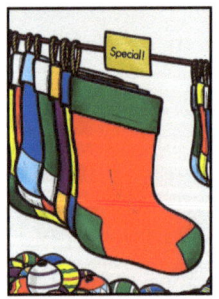

Show Illustration #2

First of all, Peggy knew the real meaning of Christmas. She knew that it was the one day when people celebrated the birthday of Jesus. And she knew everyone hustled about getting trees trimmed, presents wrapped in pretty packages, lots and lots of cookies made, and went to special services in the church. But it was not until several days before Christmas that Peggy began to think about hanging stockings on the mantle on Christmas Eve.

Show Illustration #3

Peggy saw lovely BIG bright colored stockings in the department store. She hoped Mommy would buy one for her with PEGGY written across the top in lovely "glittery" letters. Peggy saw pictures of boys and girls emptying Christmas stockings. One little girl had a beautiful doll sticking right out of the top of her stocking. And the little boy in the picture had his stocking already emptied. He had found toy cars, trains, candy, and a great big fat orange in his. Peggy could scarcely wait to go and buy hers.

The night before Mommy and Peggy were to go to the store, Peggy's Daddy took his little girl on his lap. "It seems to me my little girl is quite excited about Christmas," he said.

Peggy's blue eyes shone. "I am going to have a Christmas stocking with my name on it," she said. Daddy held his daughter close as he told her again how the Lord Jesus left heaven, where He was very rich, and came to earth where He was very poor. "He did not have to come," Daddy said. "He did it because He loves us, Peggy. He wanted to take the punishment for our sins so we can go to Heaven and live with Him; for He went back to Heaven after He was crucified and rose again.

"It is at Christmas time that we remember about Jesus' coming down to be born as a baby. His mother held Him in her arms, just as I am holding you. Only He was brand new, born that very first Christmas.

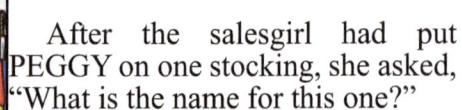

Show Illustration #4

"Poor Baby Jesus," Peggy said drowsily, "no one hung up a stocking for Him."

Then she sat up, suddenly wide awake. "Mommy!" she called to her mother "Let's hang up a stocking for Baby Jesus, too."

The next day, Peggy and her mommy went to the store to get the stockings. Peggy chose a stocking for herself and one for Jesus. Mother was ready to pay for the stockings and have them, wrapped. But Peggy protested. "Mommy, we have to have names on the stockings."

Show Illustration #5

After the salesgirl had put PEGGY on one stocking, she asked, "What is the name for this one?"

Mommy hesitated for a moment. "JESUS," Peggy whispered.

"Put JESUS on that one," Mommy told the salesgirl.

Show Illustration #6

Thinking she had misunderstood, the salesgirl said, "What is the name, please?"

When Mother answered, the salesgirl looked at her strangely. And so Mother had to explain

– 26 –

about the stocking for Jesus being Peggy's idea because it was really Jesus' birthday. The salesgirl smiled as she wrote in large glittery letters, JESUS.

That was just the beginning of many explanations, for Peggy insisted on hanging Jesus' stocking up right away. She would not wait for Christmas. And so the visitors who came to the home heard the story about *Peggy's Christmas Stocking for Jesus*. Peggy told the milkman, the postman, and everyone who came to the house about Jesus' stocking.

Show Illustration #7

Of course, everyone who heard the story wanted to put a gift in the stocking for JESUS. And so it came about that the stocking finally had $13.87 in it. After Christmas was over, Mommy said, "Now we had better get this present off to Jesus. We cannot send it to Him up in heaven. But we can give it to him by giving it to some Christian worker, perhaps some missionary. You may decide where to give Jesus' present, dear."

Show Illustration #8

Peggy thought and thought for several days. Her grownup friends had many suggestions to make. But it was Peggy who finally said, "I want to give it to Aunt Beryl. Lots of boys and girls get to hear about Jesus because she works all the time for Him."

And so it was that the money from the stocking Peggy had hung up for Jesus was used that boys and girls in Pennsylvania might know that He had died for them. And many grown-ups, including the postman and the milkman, heard again the true meaning of Christmas.

* * * * * * * *

Suggestion: In your Sunday school class or home Bible class, hang a stocking with the name JESUS on it. Encourage the children to place their missionary offerings in it each week during the month of December.

www.ingramcontent.com/pod-product-compliance
Lightning Source LLC
Chambersburg PA
CBHW060804090426
42736CB00002B/158